Your Pets Best Life

I0178137

NOW!!

5 Simple Steps to Successful Pet Ownership

The sale of this book without the cover is unauthorized.

If you purchased this book without a cover, you should be aware that it was reported to the publisher as "unsold and destroyed." Neither the author nor the publisher has received payment for a "stripped book."

Copyright © 2015 by De'Monica Cooper Amerson

All rights reserved. No part of this publication in whole or in part, or stored in a retrieval system, or transmitted in any form or by any means, without written permission of the publisher.

For information regarding permission, write to Imagine Me Publishing, Attention Publication Department imaginemeinc@yahoo.com

ISBN: 978-0-9845393-2-1

Printed in the U.S.A.

About The Book

This book was inspired by many individuals. Mostly those whom I've had the unfortunate task of explaining the extent of emergency medical care that is needed to treat their pet. Many of these individuals never thought this could happen to their pet. To say the least, their pet being in an Emergency Critical Care situation was definitely not a part of the plan.

After seeing this happen over and over again, a thought, no a scripture came to mind,

Hosea 4:6 "My people are destroyed from lack of knowledge."

This scripture allowed me to see things from a different perspective.

The people that bring their animals in for emergency treatment are not bad owner's, they are just uninformed owners.

I asked God if He would bless me to be a blessing to write a book that would help perspective pet owner's to be better informed about being responsible pet owners.

And even after being informed, "**things do just happen**." And when they happen, you being a responsible pet owner should and/or must be prepared for minor and major emergencies. I can't stress enough "**things happen**", and you must respond responsively.

FYI.... Pet ownership is a choice and not a necessity.

When informed choices are made, things tend to work out. Keep in mind that everything you own costs something. When working with something **Alive,** the cost generally tends to be more.

When you love something, you tend to do **more** for it and in most cases; there is no limit as to what you are willing to do to show your love. We show this in caring, pampering and spending a little extra on our pets. We really go all out! The way we treat our pets today, has changed a great deal. We really love them and they are a part of the family. We live indoors, they live indoors. *There is no such thing as an outside pet.*

We buy them clothes, special food, treats and yes, they have their own bed. Yes, pet ownership has changed and changed for the better! My prayer is that after you read this book, you, the reader will be well prepared for successful pet ownership.

Proverbs 12:10, "The righteous care for the needs of their animals."

Until One Has Loved an Animal, Part of Their Soul Remains Unwakened…

Unknown

Contents

Preparation Is Everything

In a world where all types of information is available right under our fingertips, it's amazing how we haphazardly decide to become pet owners. More thought and a lot of research should be put into the idea. You can't wake up one morning and say, **"Hey I think a pet would be a great addition to this family",** without talking to your family first, and doing some extensive research. Treat it as if you're buying your dream house or that fancy new Beemer X5 you've been eyeing at the BMW dealership. These things have been on your mind for a while and you know exactly what to expect once you've acquired them. Maintenance, possible repairs, insurance etc....the same holds true when deciding on pet ownership. The family has to sit down and talk about it. Especially when children are involved. Remember, children can't pay for anything, even though their opinions are welcomed, and they will give you very good reasons as to why they need a pet, don't let that be the deciding factor. You the parent will be the responsible one. So with that in mind don't get all googly-eyed and mushy –hearted when you see the excitement on your child's or children's face at the mention of owning a pet.

Seriously... have a family meeting. During your family meeting calculate the amount of time you all may or may not have to give to a pet. Take into consideration any pet, no matter how large or small, will always have a need. Adults, it's ok to wait if you're not sure. Do not allow the stereotype of the complete family package; spouse, house, children, and pet; be the deciding factor on owning a pet.

After your family meeting and before making any final decisions, remember there are things that still need to be researched and considered.

Some of those things to consider are:

How will the pet be housed while you're at work and school?

Do you keep it in a kennel or a small room?

How will the pet respond to being in a kennel all day? Believe it or not some pets have anxiety issues.

How do you know that your new pet isn't that one?

Will your new pet whine and or howl all day while you're gone?

Will your pet be able to not make a mess in its kennel while waiting on you to get home?

Who's responsible for cleaning the pet's kennel or area where the pet will be housed?

Is there a space in your home that can be designated for the pet?

Does your apartment complex allow animals and if so are there breed restrictions/weight limits?

Is there a place on the property designated for pets to be walked?

What type of pet will work best with your family?

Canine or Feline? Puppy or Kitten?

What happens if after acquiring your pet, the pet doesn't quite fit with your family?

Let's say after you've had the pet a couple of months you decide that your family is not ready for pet ownership, what happens to the pet?

FYI...there are no do over's in pet ownership. That is why it's so important to try and get it right the first time.

Here's another very important question that should only be

discussed between those individuals that will be making financial decisions pertaining to your new pet.

Have you considered the **TOTAL** cost of pet ownership? Not just the initial purchase of the pet, but long term.

Your time

Socialization & Training

 Love

Unconditional

Finances

Vaccines, Heartworm, Flea and Tick preventatives, Grooming, Food, Pet Insurance etc...

In addition to the extra items we choose to buy to spoil our pets. Believe me, there will be a lot of spoiling going on. Definitely money well spent. Remember, your pet has needs that only you can provide.

For those single individuals who are considering pet ownership, you will have to be more conscience of the time you spend away from home. A dog can only hold their bladder for so long and when their limit is reached, rest assured there will be an accident waiting for you to clean when you get home.

Cats on the other hand have access to their litter box, but you could still come home to not an accident, but an incident, because someone may have missed you. I'm not saying your fun has to stop, just make sure to incorporate time to go home and take care of your pet. It lets your pet know that when you leave, you will only be gone for a short time and you haven't abandoned them. Having a pet can give you a sense of being responsible for something other than yourself. And it also makes you responsible for this life. And we all know there's nothing better than being a responsible pet owner. Over time, your pet becomes a part of the family. I can't give you an exact length of time when it happens, but it happens.

One day as you're relaxing on the couch watching television or just enjoying some quiet time. You glance over at your puppy or kitten and realize your pet has developed into an adult dog or cat, and you ask yourself, "when did that happen?" As you continue looking at your pet, you take a quick walk down memory lane; a big smile comes over your face as you remember those days of them being a puppy or kitten (painful at times). You shake your head and realize that somehow along the way they've acquired a special place in your heart and home. It's at that moment, you know your cat or dog is more than just a pet, and it is a member of the family. The joy of pet ownership has arrived and you my friend are smack dab in the middle of it.

Whew Whoo!!!

And those are just a few thoughts about puppy and kitten ownership.

Let's move on to the toddler /preteen stage.

Now that your pet has reached a certain level of maturity (not much) the level of care changes. It includes more involvement on your part. When I say more involvement, I mean it's time to lay down the law; yours and not theirs. Don't get me wrong, you've been very successful in teaching them to sleep in their overpriced kennel with matching bed and not outside of it on the cold floor. You've aced potty training with little to no accidents. Yay You!!! You've almost got them trained to not stare you and company in the face with that pitiful look until you give them anything you are eating. All those things are great and very much needed, but you are about to enter into a different playing field. And if you don't play the game right, life as you've known it could change.

Always remember "You're in charge, not the pet."

What follows next?

I would call this the "let's see what I can get away with" stage for the pet. Just as a baby grows from infancy to toddler, they become more aware of their surroundings, their level of confidence is increasing, and before you know it they are walking, talking and getting into everything. Well the same things happen with your pet. Your pet still isn't sure what's happening. In their mind, I imagine them saying, "Wow, it's all kinds of stuff for me to get into in this house." So as you notice that your pet is venturing out more and listening less **Keep an eye on them!**

This is also the time to interact with them and make the necessary changes to ensure your pet is well disciplined. Remember, an animal's attention span is limited. So if you didn't see them do the deed, don't discipline them. You don't want to confuse your pet. Make sure you are firm with your discipline, but not too harsh. You want your pet to know you mean business, but at the same time you don't want your pet afraid of you. **Keep an eye on them!**

Make the necessary changes that will ensure the safety of the pet. Things will need to be child/ animal proofed. Don't leave anything laying on the floor, bed, bathroom, kitchen, etc. If they can see it, they will figure out a way to get it.

Set boundaries

If you don't want them to have access to certain rooms in the home, never introduce them to that room. If you don't want them on your furniture, don't show them how to jump on the couch or bed. Don't fool yourself; animals really do understand the words that come out of our mouth. If you have doubts, ask anyone that has ever been apprehended by HPD's K-9 unit. When their handler releases the chain leash from the dogs' harness and says, "go to work," the dog does not come back empty handed. Teach your pet whatever you want and need them to know and do. Do so with just the right amount of firmness, and you'll be glad you implemented discipline as a part of your daily routine. Just to recap, responsible pet ownership is not all fun and games, but if done right, the benefits are rewarding. After the newness wears off and things have settled, reality sets in. And you have to be committed to doing your best at becoming a responsible pet owner. I can't stress this enough,

KEEP AN EYE ON THEM!!!!!

And definitely **Do Your Research FIRST!!!**

Adoption, Purchase or Rescue?

Well if you've made it this far, good for you! The decision to get a pet has been discussed with all members of the family, young and old. But, most importantly, approved by the adults. Yay You!

Now the question is **Adoption, Purchase or Rescue?**

Each option has its pros and cons, just so you are aware. Whichever one you decide to use, just make sure it works for you and your family.

Here's more important information you should know, starting with **Adoption** and **Rescue**, which are somewhat one in the same with a slight twist.

Adoption is usually from a facility like S.P.C.A., B.A.R.C. or The Humane Society. Your local pet store may work with different entities to help get stray animals placed in good homes. These animals that are now in the care of one or more of these facilities are unusually put there by individuals who may have had to relocate for their job and were not in a position to take the pet with them. It's possible the previous owner may have recently experienced something life changing and they were no longer in a position to give their pet the best care. Or the ultimate reason, the owner is deceased and there was no one available to care for the pet.

For whatever reason quite a few pets do end up in some type of facility. The outcome is more certain but not good for those animals that do. The reason being is there tends to be more stray animals then there are good homes.

Rescue groups on the other hand do work in the same capacity, but often the majority of animals that are found, usually are roaming the streets looking for food, water and shelter. Many may have been injured, HBC (hit by car), or have health issues that the owner couldn't afford or maybe health care wasn't an option. There are many reasons as to why and how an animal becomes a stray. Prayerfully, this book can and will help prevent any animal from becoming a stray. There are also special cases where the animal may have experienced some type of trauma or abuse. In cases of reported abuse, animals can and will be removed from the situation. Some rescue groups work with different facilities and when an adoptable animal has not been adopted within a certain time limit for that facility, a rescue worker will get this information and pick the animal up from the facility. Unfortunately, this doesn't happen too often. From my experience most stray pets are abandoned by their owners, found roaming the streets and left alone to fend for themselves. If you are no longer able to give your pet a safe, loving, and caring home it's okay to turn them over to any shelter or rescue group. It's much better than the alternative... a pet being left alone and afraid.

Here's a scenario on how rescue groups work.

A rescue worker has noticed a dog that has recently given birth roaming the street in a certain neighborhood. The worker will check the dog out for a few days, maybe leave food out for the dog, with hopes of gaining trust from the dog and eventually interact with the dog. The stray dog is aware of the worker's presence over the past few days; the dog readily comes up to the worker. The worker then feels confident that the dog is ready for contact. The dog is then picked up and taken into the rescue worker's home. Once trust has been established by both parties, the worker readily takes the mother into his or her home, gives her food, water and shelter and would then go back to find the pups and bring them in as well, care for them and later find homes for them all. This actually happens quite often more with dogs than cats. This is due to the fact that cats are very independent. VERY.... even in bleak situations, cats can and will refuse to be helped. When cats have had little to no interaction with people it's called "Feral". The cats are wild and untamed, and usually stay together in what is called a "Colony." Because it takes much longer to gain their trust and vice versa, some people will not interact with feral cats other than to ensure they have fresh food and water. I know it sounds a bit cruel, but it works really well for both parties.

I mentioned trust earlier because animals much like people, can be in a very bleak situation and still not know or be unsure of the motive of the person who's offering the help they need. You have to have genuine concern, patience, and a loving heart to be a rescue worker. There must be something about you that says "I'm here to help."

Rescue workers are out looking for strays daily and often find them. Many animals are available to be adopted through rescue groups and some rescue groups are breed specific. So if you're looking for a specific breed, I suggest checking Google for that breed to see what is available. While information about the animal can and probably will be limited due to the nature of the rescue, don't be discouraged, just try to get as much present information as you can from the individual or individuals who fostered the pet. An animal that can't be placed into a home due to past trauma or abuse usually ends up staying with the foster. Some pets may just need more time to trust again.

A rescue animal can be in the care of a foster anywhere from 5 days to 5 years or longer. The goal is to take care of the pet until it is healthy physically, emotionally, and is ready to be placed in good home.

What to expect from your rescued pet? Your rescue pet should have had a series of vaccs, if not all of them depending on age. Deworming is a plus to have as well. Having their first dose of heartworm and flea/ tick prevention as well as being spayed or neutered are expected. Paperwork please...verbal vaccine history without proof is comparable to no vaccines.

Some very important things to know or questions to ask are:

The present history of that particular pet while in the care of the facility or foster.

Why was the pet placed in an Adoption or Rescue facility?

How long was it in its original owners care?

Age?

Compatibility with children and other animals?

Has it ever bitten or attacked anyone or another animal while in the care of the facility or foster?

In rescue situations, the number of individuals dealing with the pet will be limited to only a few volunteers. The foster will probably have other foster animals in the home and will have had this pet in their care for a

good amount of time. The goal is to get a feel of how the pet interacts with other animals and people.
In my personal opinion adoption /rescue are equally important. Rescuing an animal off the streets, providing proper health care, food/water, and just the right amount of love gives an animal just what is needed to become that special pet that God created it to be. But, if you're not completely sold on adoption or rescue, definitely go ahead and purchase a pet for your family.

The Cost of Pet Ownership

The cost of pet ownership consists of 2 major things: **Finances and Time**

Let's talk about **finances** first. You've done your research on the particular breed that interests you. By research I mean you went online, possibly bought a book or two on your future pet. You know the behind the scene stuff, not some worthless information you may have gotten from the guy who knows something about everything and nothing about breed specification. Your research has provided you with valuable information such as life expectancy. It's common knowledge that small breed dogs live longer. Smush nosed animals have breathing issues. What diseases are common in your pet of choice? These are just a few things you should know beforehand. I say this because if you only saved enough money for the initial purchase, that first visit to the Vet will make you rethink your decision about pet ownership. If you purchase from a breeder, whether in town or out, your window of opportunity is narrow. What I mean by this is, once the puppy leaves the breeder and is now in your custody, the clock has started ticking. You have a certain amount of time to get it seen by a Vet, hopefully by your regular Vet because you are a responsible Pet owner and did the responsible thing and chose a vet for your new pet. Enough about being a responsible pet owner, I know you guys are responsible by now. This is where your research comes in handy. You've been speaking with the breeder on a regular basis and you've established some type of relationship. Good for you!

So there's a level of trust between you and the breeder. Great! It's all about you the pet owner making the best informed decision. If you purchase the pet over the weekend, take it to the Vet on Monday, Tuesday at the latest for a checkup. You need to know the current health condition of the animal you just purchased.

FYI:

You can have all the necessary paperwork that says this animal is healthy, but until you, the actual pet owner takes your new pet to have an exam with your regular Vet, there is no guarantee of the healthiness of your new pet. Then and only then can you be sure that your new pet is really healthy. Unfortunately, a lot of the times this is not the case. New pet owners are so excited about their new pet that when they take it home and get comfortable with the pet they pretty much forget about the visit.

Let's say it's now Saturday, the puppy has been fine all week, eating and drinking, just being a rambunctious puppy. Then the puppy won't eat or drink and you're not sure when the last time it had anything to eat or drink. It's vomiting and having diarrhea, is lethargic and listless, and you may even think it's no longer breathing. In that instant you realize that something is seriously wrong with your new pet. What do you do? Not sure. Here's a hint.....Emergency Care Hospital here we come. Emergency care at this point is a MUST!!! From this point on and going forward, you've reached a different level.

The Reality of Pet Ownership

Right here and right now. You've become a responsible pet owner. Even though this could have been avoided... you have made the right decision to get your pet medical attention. The difference in medical treatment at this point is, now your pet is sick and tests will have to be done to diagnosis what's going on with your pet. Please keep in mind, the cost of emergency care is probably double what you would pay at your regular vet. Just like in human medicine, you are paying for emergency medical care. So don't go into sticker shock when you're presented with an estimate to care for your pet. This is why that initial vet exam is so important. The only health information you have on your pet is what information that was given to you by the breeder. Which is not very helpful now? Your regular vet would have done a complete physical exam. This exam includes listening to the heart for abnormalities, lungs to make sure they are clear. Palpating (feeling) the abdomen, bladder, looking in the ears and looking at the eyes, and in the mouth for any abnormalities. The skin gets a once over as well. If all checks out, your Vet will then give vaccines, but only if the pet is of age. Heartworm and flea prevention will be a lifelong thing that you do for your pet especially if you live in Texas. Heartworms are transmitted from mosquitoes, and fleas transmit tapeworms. This exam/ first visit to your vet is very important in the well-being of your pet. So please be compliant. This way you'll know for yourself that your pet is healthy or if it may have health issues. In either case, knowing helps to make educated responsible decisions about your pet's health.

Time is very important. You must take the right amount of time necessary to get to know your pet physically. When you spend time playing, holding, cuddling or just allowing the pet to sit on your lap, take that time to do a quick exam. What you're feeling for is the texture of the fur, soft or rough. Thick or fine, any lumps or bumps. Anything that just doesn't feel right. This way you will easily know when things are different with your pet's skin and fur. Don't forget to use your nose. I'm sure you're thinking "What is she talking about my nose?" Yes, your nose. Many different illnesses have a distinct smell. To give you a few examples, infected ears have a yeasty smell. Some skin issues smell wet, sweaty and a lot like Fritos. Any type of abscess smells like rotting flesh. When a pet is having urinary problems the urine has a specific odor. Renal disease makes the urine have a sweet (so not good) smell. Dental disease can cause your pets breath to smell bad. Another bad smell coming from your pet could be anal glands. An animal's anal glands should automatically express when your pet has a bowel movement. If you see your pet scooting their butt across the floor, *it's not a new trick they've learned*, they are trying to express their anal glands. If this action is done on a regular basis, you may want to have your regular Vet exam your pet for this issue. A ruptured anal gland is not only smelly to you, but it is also very painful for your pet. These are just a few things you can do to better know your pet's physical health condition. Also you may want to keep a journal of your pet's health issues. If you ever have to take your pet to the EC, knowing your pets previous and existing health issue will be a great help in diagnosing your pets' current emergency. Even though you are not a vet, you can exam your pet physically, just by frequently petting and rubbing your pet, looking in your pet's mouth, paying close attention to the teeth and gum line. Make sure all the baby teeth are out and his adult teeth are in place. Most definitely get your pet use to having its mouth opened and handled. Playfully place your hand in its mouth, just be careful and don't get bitten. If you make this a part of the routine you have with your pet, you'll be the first to know if and when something changes with your pet's health. Play with your pet's feet, your pet needs to be okay with you or anyone touching their feet, especially your regular vet and the technicians. Rub the head, look in the ears. You may never know when or if you may have to medicate your pet for an ear infection or a cut on the paw or broken toenail. Believe me, it will be much easier for you to medicate your pet, if the pet is used to having your hands in his mouth, so to speak.

Interact, Interact, and Interact with your pet!!! The amount of interaction between you, your family and your pet is very important. Not just for socialization reasons, but so your pet feels loved and cared for. All your pet wants is to give love and be loved in return.

So as you see, pet ownership cannot be a spur of the moment decision. It cost both time and finance. Pet ownership is a luxury that doesn't work well for everyone. And that's ok!!!!

Check list for Pet Owners

1. Choose a pet that will best fit the needs of your family.

2. Make sure you are ready for the newest member of your family.

3. Have you acquired some type of pet insurance or do you have sufficient funds saved and available in case of an emergency.

4. Have a regular Vet.

5. Take your pet in for regular checkups.

6. Keep your pet on heartworm and flea prevention year round, especially if you live in Texas.

7. Have you pet spayed or neutered if it's not already altered.

8. There is no such thing as an outside pet.

Epilogue

I would also like to add:

As you continue working to become a responsible pet owner, don't over react when things happen. What you may deem as an emergency may not be in the eyes of the experts. Unless there is profuse vomiting, bleeding, bone exposure, eyeball out of socket, difficulty breathing, non-responsiveness, just to name a few, it's possible your pet may not need immediate emergency medical attention. An ear infection *(unless it's discharging any type of fluid)* would not be considered an emergency. A toenail trim because your cat keeps scratching you and your expensive rug or furniture, is not an emergency.

For non-emergency things, go to your Regular Vet and let him or her do their job, and that's taking care of your pet.

Another thing, if you've noticed that your pet is not behaving normally, don't wait days before you take it in to be seen by your vet. Time is of the essence when your pet is sick. When you wait too long, that minor issue a few days ago will most likely now be a major issue. Which in turn will be more expensive for you? My suggestion if your pet is not doing well in the morning; drop it off at your regular vet on your way to work. This way the pet is being monitored and not at home all day getting worse. Communicate with your regular vet and the staff. Call and let them know that your pet is doing this or not doing that. If the vet feels that it can wait until the following day, wait. But if your pet gets worse and can't wait until the next morning, don't hesitate to get it medical attention.

One last piece of information I'd like to share. Don't self-diagnosis your pet, its wrong when we do it to ourselves. Get your pet checked out by your vet, and not some website on the internet. The internet didn't go to veterinary school and it should only be used as a tool to help you understand the "what if's, and could be's". Learn to trust your regular Vet and always have an Emergency Medical Plan in place for your pet.

If you have finished reading this book you are now a...

Successful, Responsible Pet Owner!

www.ingramcontent.com/pod-product-compliance
Lightning Source LLC
Chambersburg PA
CBHW071648040426
42452CB00009B/1810

* 9 7 8 0 9 8 4 5 3 9 3 2 1 *